Original Korean text by Min-hui Jeon
Illustrations by Seong-geun Muhn
Korean edition © Dawoolim

This English edition published by big & SMALL in 2015
by arrangement with Dawoolim
English text edited by Joy Cowley
English edition © big & SMALL 2015

ISBN: 978-1-925234-07-7

Printed in Korea

Special Environments

Written by Min-hui Jeon
Illustrated by Seong-geun Muhn
Edited by Joy Cowley

big & SMALL

The earth we live on, has
tropical rainforests thick with trees,
deserts covered with sand,
polar regions with freezing
cold ice and deep oceans.

Tundra

Tropical
rainforest

Arctic

Desert

Antarctic

Tropical rainforest* is an environment that is found in hot and wet regions in the tropical regions near the equator. They cover about 6% of the world's surface.

* Tropical rainforests exist in southeastern Asia, northeastern Australia, Sri Lanka, central Africa, South America, Central America and on many of the Pacific Islands.

Toucan

Pigmy marmoset monkey

The top of the tropical rainforest

The top layers of rainforest
look like green umbrellas.
Branches grow into each other,
providing homes for animals and birds.

King vulture

Macaw

Squirrel monkey

The middle of the tropical rainforest

The trees grow close together,
blocking much of the light.
Vines and branches make bridges
for many animals.

Sloth

Spider monkey

Long-armed ape

The floor of the tropical rainforest

On the dim, wet forest floor
grow numerous plants.
Animals roam around
looking for food.

Giant ant-eater

Iguana

Jaguar

Armadillo

Hummingbird

Rivers of the tropical rainforest

Big rivers flow through the trees.
When fierce animals appear,
timid animals run away.

Tapir

Basilisk

Anaconda

Alligator

A desert* is a very dry region of land where there is little precipitation (rain, snow, mist or fog) or because more water is lost by evaporation than falls. The annual rainfall is less than 250mm.
There are sandy deserts and non-sandy deserts.

Camel

*Among the largest deserts are Sahara Desert (in Africa), Arabian Desert (in Middle East), Gobi Desert (in Asia), Patagonian Desert (in South America), Great Victorian Desert (in Australia), Kalahari Desert (in Africa) and Great Basin Desert (North America).

Sand dunes in the desert

There is very little rain in the desert.
Wind blows the sand into high ridges.
Animals and plants have adapted
to an environment of hot, dry sand.

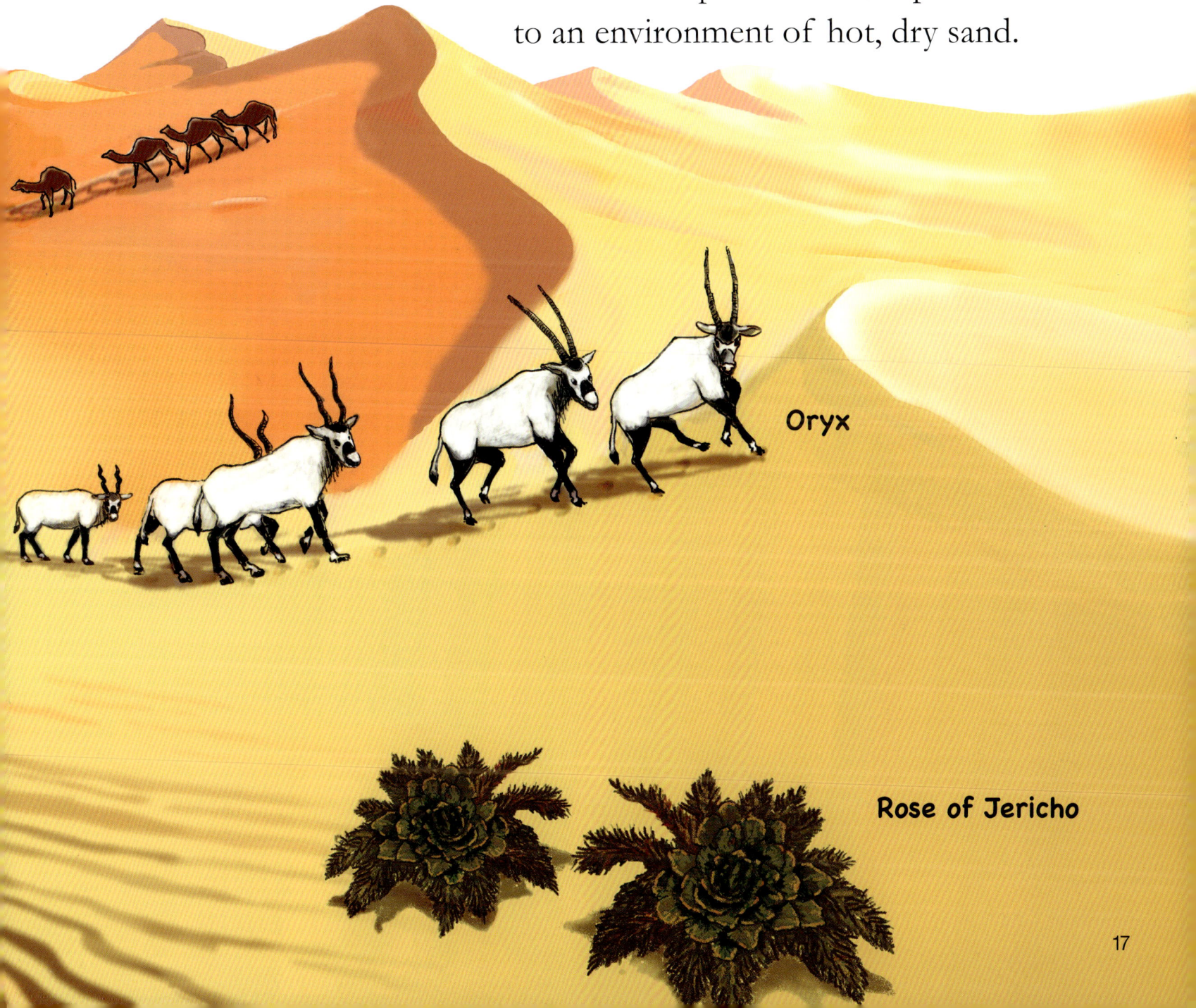

Oryx

Rose of Jericho

An oasis in the desert

Even in barren deserts, there are springs.
Such a spring is called an oasis.
Palm trees and reeds grow around the water.
Animals can eat and drink.

Desert grasshopper

Oryx

Kangaroo rat

Scorpion

Fennec fox

A cactus in the desert

Some deserts have cacti living in groups.
Some cacti are small, some are very tall.
A cactus can store water in its stem.
Owls shelter from the blazing sun
in old hollow cacti.

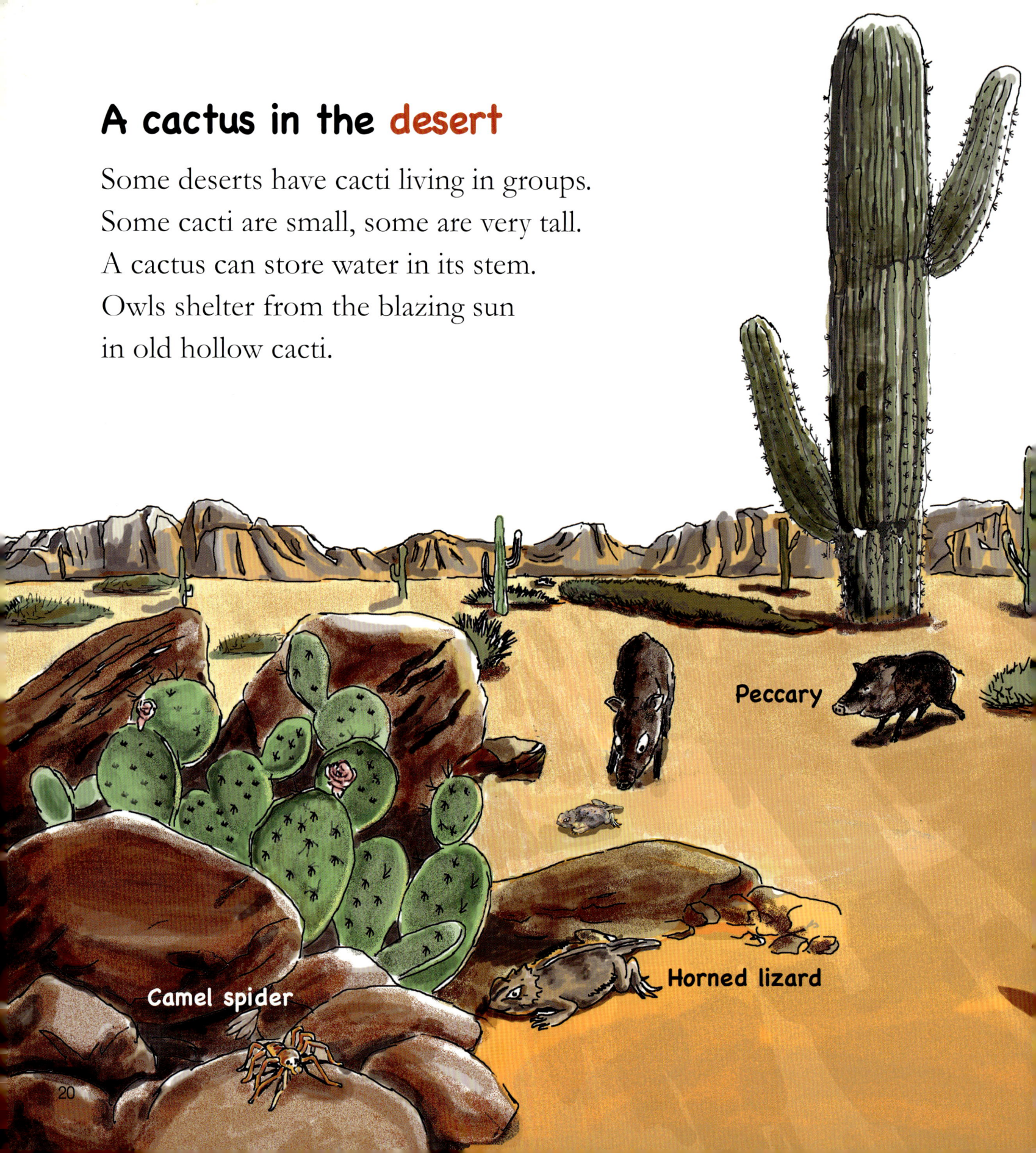

Peccary

Horned lizard

Camel spider

Elf owl

Cactus →

Black-tailed jackrabbit

The Arctic* is the polar region in the northernmost part of Earth. It has two seasons: cold winter and cool summer. The average winter temperature is -40°C.

*The Arctic consists of the Arctic Ocean and parts of Alaska (USA), Canada, Iceland, Greenland (Denmark), Finland, Norway, Sweden and Russia, surrounding the Arctic Ocean.

Elephant seal

Leopard seal

Sabine's gull

The freezing cold Arctic

The Arctic has many icebergs and glaciers*.
These enormous bodies of ice move very slowly,
and can double in size during the winter.

*Icebergs and glaciers are also found in the Antarctic.
Scientists believe that ice in the Arctic and Antarctic region is
melting rapidly in the recent years because of global warming.

Arctic fox

Polar bear

The treeless land, Tundra

The land around the polar regions is called tundra.
The soil in tundra is mostly frozen, so trees can not
grow there. Only mosses and small plants can grow.
But in summer, there are flowers and berries.

* Tundra regions are located at the edges of the
Artic and Antarctic regions.

Musk-ox

Arctic poppy

Arctic wolf

Reindeer

The Antarctic is the other polar region on Earth. It consists of Antarctica, Earth's southernmost continent and the Southern Ocean.

Adelie penguin

Emperor penguin

Vega gull

The land of snow and ice, Antarctica

Antarctica is the coldest, driest and windiest land in the world. It is frozen all year round. Penguins nest and raise their young on the land of snow and ice.

Seal

The Southern Ocean

The Southern Ocean surrounds Antarctica.
A small red shrimp called krill lives
in the Southern Ocean. Millions of them drift
in swarms that provide food
for whales, penguins and sea birds.

Krill

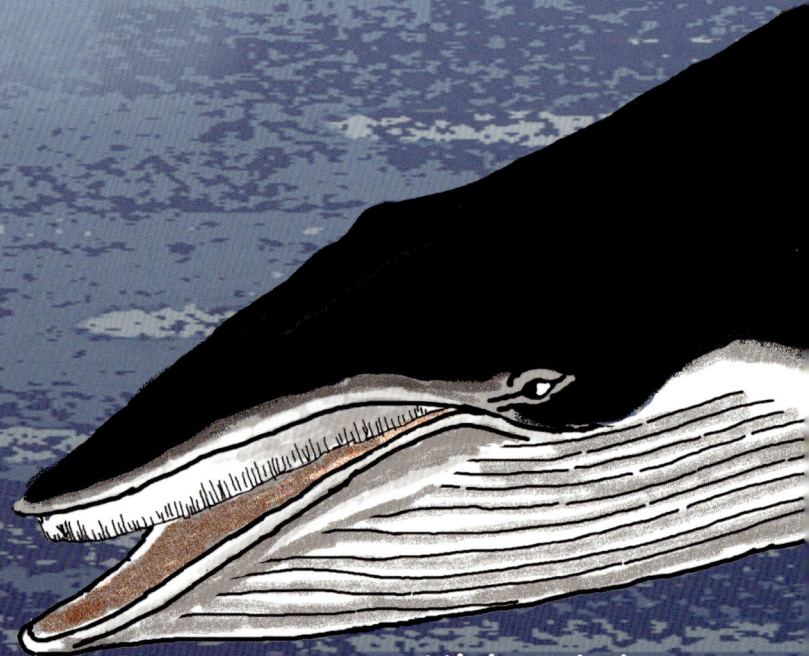

Minke whale

Starfish

Antarctic cod

Sea urchin

Squid

Special natural environments

The Earth has many different environments, varying in temperature, weather, geographic features and many other factors. Different plants and animals have adapted to live in each environment. The special environments in this book are outside of the warm temperate regions where most of the world's population lives.

Let's think!

What are the main environments found on Earth?

What are some of the reasons why different regions of the globe have different environments?

How do animals and plants adapt to their environment?

Let's do!

Choose one of the Earth's environments to study closely. Do research using your library or the Internet to find out as much as you can. On a piece of paper write down:

- The name of the environment
- The locations it can be found
- The weather
- Other special features of the environment
- Animals and plants that live there
- Anything else interesting that you discover in your research